# EMPTINESS

Robert Wolfe

Karina Library Press
2020

*Emptiness*
by Robert Wolfe

ISBN: 978-1-937902-35-3

Library of Congress LCCN: 2020951015

Karina Library Press
Michael Lommel, publisher
PO Box 35
Ojai, California
93024
www.karinalibrary.com

Manuscript preparation: Dr. Bobbi Liberton

*A grateful dedication
to Tom Rohn.*

In my favorite story about Ramana Maharshi, a man came into the room where Ramana held satsang, said he'd written a biography of Ramana and asked permission to read it. Ramana smiled and nodded, and the man read his manuscript.

It was full of inaccuracies and error: he said that Ramana was married and had children, that he'd been a Socialist before his enlightenment, and on and on.

When he finished reading, Ramana smiled and nodded, and the man picked up his manuscript and left.

One of Ramana's disciples cried out, "Master, did you hear what he read? Is any of that real?!"

Ramana waved his hand as if taking in the universe, and asked: "Is any of *this* real?"

Robert Wolfe

*Living Nonduality*

*Abiding in Nondual Awareness*

*Awakening to Infinite Presence*

*Always—Only—One*

*Ramana Maharshi: The Teachings of Self-realization*

*One Essence*

*Science of the Sages*

*The Enlightenment Teachings of Jesus*

www.ajatasunyata.com

www.livingnonduality.org

# Preface

This is definitely not a book to reinforce your ideas of who you think you are. If anything, it is about who you *aren't*, to the ultimate degree. It *is* about how one lives one's life, despite the fact that we don't, in reality, have one. The viewpoint of ajata turns one's "world" upside down. It reorients even our view of life and death.

Since my awakening, thirty-one years ago, I have been teaching precepts of nonduality, or advaita.

Advaita points one toward the deepest implication of spirituality; the vedanta tradition used *ajata* to name that, the buddhist tradition used *sunyata*. We call it *emptiness*.

I examined over eighty books on the source material of emptiness to see how sages (and scholars) had attempted to communicate or understand it. Most had something worthwhile to say, but none told the complete story in a single book.

— RW

*Like water in a mirage, a dream, an echo, a phantom emanation, a reflection, a castle in the air or a hallucination, all things are clearly apparent yet do not truly exist.*

*Although they do not exist, they appear to, and in manifesting they have no basis.*

Longchenpa

# Ajata/Sunyata

*Ajata* is a Sanskrit word meaning no creation; that is, no origination.

Hui Neng, the Sixth Chinese Patriarch, summed up the point of view of ajata when he said, in the last two lines of his enlightenment poem:

> Where there has been nothing from the start
> how can dust alight?

*Sunyata* (also spelled shunyata) is a Sanskrit word, older than the Buddha, meaning emptiness.

Where there is nothing from the start, there is emptiness. Or, where there is emptiness, not anything can be originated—there is nothing from the start.

Ajata is a term associated with Advaita Vedanta. Sunyata is a term associated with Buddhism.

Both Advaita Vedanta and Buddhism have their roots in India. Buddha's teachings on emptiness were the subject of a school of writers known largely as *Madhyamaka* (also spelled Madhyamika), who embraced the writings of the Indian monk Nagarjuna, from around 200 A.D.

The ajata of the Indian nonduality teacher Guadapada and the sunyata of the Indian monk Chandrakirti (or

Candrakirti), around 600 A.D., were evidently an influence on each other.

The point of these teachings is that the basic condition, or "ultimate reality", is emptiness. Not any reality (or dharma) has ever had a beginning. Therefore, anything which is *supposed* to exist, or be real, is in truth without substance. While things may appear to be real, all appearances are empty, and therefore have no true existence beyond their appearance. In other words, life as we think we know it is purely an illusion.

Not anything has ever been created, or born. To the person who supposes that his life and death and the turmoil of this world are real, the realization of the truth of emptiness has little appeal.

But those to whom an enlightened realization is the climax of life, emptiness is the final end to which nonduality points.

There is much written material on enlightenment, in both Vedanta and Buddhism, but—due likely to the difficulty of communicating such a difficult subject—the sources for material on emptiness are not abundant.

Yet as the teachings of nonduality become more prominent in the West and the result is a greater number of the awakened, material on emptiness will be more widely sought.

# Ajata is...?

*Advaita* is difficult to discuss; *ajata* is infinitely more so.

Advaita tells us that reality is "not two". Ajata tells us that it is "not even one".

Ajata translates as "no creation". This means to say that nowhere has anything ever come into being. Therefore, the entire universe (or universes)—and everything therein—has no reality. In other words, the ultimate condition is nothing, or nothingness.

Advaita is to ajata, as milk is to cream. In advaita, we come to realize that "all that *is*, is That," or the Absolute. Ajata is where we subsequently come to realize that there is not *even* That (or the Absolute).

Technically, from the standpoint of ajata, even *nothingness* is *non-existent*.

In the attempt to "explain" nothingness, consider that the point of view is meant to be through *your* eyes; if it is to *be* understood, it is you for whom the comprehension matters.

The first part of the comprehension is to recognize that when you draw your last breath, you will no longer know that *you* had ever lived.

Not knowing that you had ever lived, you would not

have ever known that there was even a universe (or *anything* "in" it). This includes any other "people" or consciousnesses.

You will not have known or had awareness that *anything* ever had "existence" or "nonexistence".

The second part of this comprehension of ajata is that you definitely *will* draw your last breath.

We cannot even say that the existence of you, or anything else, has been so much as a dream, because "existence" or "nonexistence" are merely classifications *within* the "dream".

It will come to be, in fact, that *everything*—which could possibly claim that it was existent—will not even know that it (or anything else) had ever existed.

When you can come to recognize that this (ajata) is true for *you*, you can recognize that it is true for everyone, every "you", everything which is said to exist.

So, the point of ajata is that not anything is ever actually real—even categories of "existent" or "nonexistent".

You will not even be aware of "nothingness" ultimately, so we cannot even call emptiness by any names (not even the Absolute).

And it is to that "void" to which ajata is pointing.

It is no wonder that it is only someone who is thoroughly conversant with advaita who can come to "understand" ajata (or "nothingness").

This *nothing* means not anything has ever ultimately existed as real. (Not even "nothingness".)

From Wikipedia, at "Ajativada" (the teachings of ajata):

> In the Vedic Nasadiya Sukta 10:129, the first line reflects Ajativada: "Then even nothingness was not, nor existence." (circa 10,000 BCE)

*There is no division into outer and inner, and no disturbance due to thoughts arising and subsiding.*

*Since neither meditation nor anything to meditate on can be discovered, there is no need to "slay the enemies" of dullness, agitation, and thought….*

*It is of no concern whether or not all thoughts and expressions are transcended….*

*It is of no concern whether or not the view to be realized has been realized….*

*With nothing having to be renounced, the potential for error is cut through as a matter of course.*

Longchenpa

# Ramana: "I teach ajata."

"Ajata means 'non-creation,'" David Godman has written. It is a philosophical or experiential standpoint that declares or knows that neither the physical world nor the person in it have ever been created. Godman writes:

> Questions about the liberation or bondage of persons are therefore inadmissible and hypothetical since the persons themselves do not really exist. They are all a complete fiction brought about by the power of defective imagination....When one...knows the truth of ajata by direct experience...such a one is sahaja nishta [experiencing sahaja]....This particular standpoint...known as ajata or non-becoming...was the only teaching that Ramana taught from his own experience.

As Muruganar, one of Ramana's most faithful disciples has said, "We have heard him say that his true teaching, firmly based on his experience, is ajata."

Regarding such teachings, Godman has written, "Almost all his ideas were radical refutations of the concepts of physical reality that most people cherish."

Ramana has said:

> *That* alone is real...which is eternal and unchanging. Was (the world) ever seen without the aid of the mind? In deep sleep, there is neither mind nor world. When awake, there is the mind and there is the world. What does this invariable concomi-

tance mean? You are familiar with the principles of inductive logic, which are considered the very basis of scientific investigation. Why do you not decide this question of the reality of the world in the light of those accepted principles of logic?

## He adds:

There is no alternative for you but to accept the world as unreal if you are seeking the truth and the truth alone.

## Ramana notes:

A dream as a dream does not permit you to doubt its reality. It is the same in the waking state, for you are unable to doubt the reality of the world which you see while you are awake. How can the mind, which has itself created the world, accept it as unreal? That is the significance of the comparison made between the world of the waking state and the dream world. Both are creations of the mind and, so long as the mind is engrossed in either, it finds itself unable to deny their reality. It cannot deny the reality of the dream world while it is dreaming and it cannot deny the reality of the waking world while it is awake.

## Adding:

If, on the contrary, you completely withdraw your mind from the world...you will find the world of which you are now aware is just as unreal as the world in which you lived in your dream....While you are dreaming, the dream was a perfectly integrated whole. That is to say, if you felt thirsty in a dream, the illusory drinking of illusory water quenched your illusory thirst. But all this was real and not illusory to you so long as you did not know that the dream *itself* was illusory. Similarly with the waking world....

Only if there is creation do we have to explain how it came about.... Whatever you see happening in the waking state happens only to the knower, and since the knower is unreal, nothing in fact ever happens.

*Contemplate that both happiness and unhappiness are non-self-existent....*

*The same is true with all phenomena. Therefore, the state of nirvana that is beyond sorrow and the sorrowful state of cyclic existence are the same in that they are both completely devoid of any true existence.*

Geshe Kelsang Gyatso

# Ajata's Message

There are three major clues you are operating within the Dream: time, space, or cause-and-effect. That is, in short, any phenomenon.

For some time now, scientists—particularly physicists and astronomers—have been concluding some strange things about our universe. For instance, astronomy professor Mark Whittle:

> The total mass/energy of the universe equals *zero*: the universe sums to nothing. This is comparable to what one associates with traditional spiritual-based cosmologies. This also gives us insight into how the universe came into being: perhaps it *came* from nothing... So the universe could come from nothing *because it is, fundamentally, nothing*.

And physicist Don Lincoln:

> According to the theory of general relativity, before the universe began expanding—before the 'bang'—all of the matter and energy of the universe was located in a single point: a sphere with *zero* size. The scientific term for this is a singularity.
>
> If all mass and energy existed in a single point, and mass and energy are equal to space-and-time times a constant, then space and time must be in a single point.

That means that there is no other space. It's not that space exists, and the singularity exists in that space and then explodes. It's that all of space exists inside the same point. And if everything exists inside that point, then it stands to reason that *nothing* is outside of that point.

This means that when the big bang occurred, the explosion didn't expand into space. It means that space was created during the expansion. There was nothing *outside* of the universe.

So, how real is the universe? It is said to have emerged—along with time, space, and the cause-and-effect which appear in them—from a point zero in size.

In other words, we have a universe which is fundamentally nothing supposedly exploding from a zero-size point in nothing. How real does that make it?

The "universe" is in the mind—and the mind itself is ephemeral. The universe is not ultimately a reality; no more so than is the mind an ultimate reality.

Bear in mind: Nothing thou art, and to nothing thou shalt return.

That is the message of ajata.

> "There is no doubt whatsoever that the universe is the merest illusion," Sri Ramana told Sivaprakasam Pillai when questioned as a young sage at the outset of his teaching career… "clearly perceive, beyond all doubt, that the phenomenal world (as an objective, independent reality) is wholly non-existent."
>
> We could list many other statements to show just how strongly Sri Ramana felt about this, but two more should suffice to drive the point: "At the level of the spiritual seeker, you have got to say

that the world is an illusion"; and, "Unless you give up the idea that world is real, your mind will always be after it."

– *Mountain Path* Journal

*Mind does not dwell in the senses,*

*Nor in the form and such, nor in between.*

*The mind is also not found inside nor outside,*

*Nor anywhere else.*

Shantideva

# Sunyata Simplified

> When shall I reveal this truth of emptiness
> To those who go to ruin through belief
> in real existence?
> — Shantideva

Madhyamaka is a name historically given to the perception of sunyata or emptiness. Famously propounded by the Buddha (c.500 B.C.), it was principally elaborated on by the Indian monk Nagarjuna (c.150 A.D.). Other Indian monks (such as Chandrakirti and Shantideva) wrote extensively about it around 600–700 A.D. These teachings have only come to the attention of the West in recent decades, thanks to translators.

Peter Della Santina writes:

> Madhyamaka virtually disappeared from the land of its origin centuries ago. Though it continued to flourish in Tibet and Mongolia, these lands were all but inaccessible to most modern scholars....
>
> The modern study of the Madhyamaka philosophy can therefore be said to have actually commenced only a scant sixty or seventy years ago... it seems that modern scholars and students who turn their attention to the study of this system would do well to see themselves as explorers seeking to uncover new areas of knowledge....
>
> Most of these treatises were destroyed by anti-Buddhist fanaticism and vandalism carried on

first by the Brahmanical Hindus and then by invading Muslims....

This is perhaps why, even today, the Madhyamaka philosophy is often misunderstood by those who are only superficially acquainted with it. The most conspicuous example of this kind of misunderstanding is the interpretation of the Madhyamaka, which is popular in some circles, as nihilism.

The realization of emptiness goes a step beyond the Absolute of the nondual Vedic teachings. Philosopher Harsh Narain:

> Madhyamika philosophy is characterized and distinguished by a no-reality attitude. It would be a sheer travesty of truth to import into it a belief in some kind of reality like the Absolute....
>
> The Madhyamika system is for freeing or purging the mind of the web of concepts and views and verbal syndrome....
>
> Nagarjuna's suggestion is that his denial of the world does not imply belief in another order of reality like the Absolute, immanent in or transcendent to phenomena....
>
> Being is positive reality and non-being is negative reality, and the Madhyamika will not recognize any reality whatsoever, positive or negative, much less the Absolute.

And Frederick Streng:

> Thus the expression of "emptiness" is not the manifestation of the Absolute reality, the revelation of the divine, but the means for dissipating the desire for such an Absolute.

## A translator has written:

> It is recorded in the Pali Canon that the Buddha foretold the disappearance of some of his most profound teachings. They would be *misunderstood* and neglected, and would fall into oblivion. "In this way," he said, "those discourses spoken by the Tathagata that are deep, deep in meaning, supramundane, dealing with emptiness, will disappear." There is no knowing whether on that occasion he was referring to the Perfection of Wisdom, but it is certain that the earliest exponents of the Mahayana believed that, with the Prajnaparamita scriptures, they were recovering a profound and long-lost doctrine. Nagarjuna seems to have been deeply implicated in this rediscovery.

## Another translator adds:

> Of Nagarjuna's life, we know almost nothing. He is said to have been born into a Brahmin family in the south of India around the beginning of the second century CE. He became a monk and a teacher of high renown and exerted a profound and pervasive influence on the evolution of the Buddhist tradition in India and beyond.

## Philosophy professor Jay Garfield:

> Nagarjuna and his followers do argue that the entire everyday world is, from the ultimate standpoint, nonexistent.

## Bill Porter (Red Pine):

> That *form* is empty was one of the Buddha's earliest and most frequent pronouncements....By the time of his nirvana in 383 B.C., there were still not many members of his order who understood this teaching or its ramifications.

## Guy Armstrong:

> The fact that so many books have been written about emptiness points to both the richness and the complexity of the subject....Awakened seeing recognizes that there is no actual "being" present anywhere, either in life or death...
>
> More than just austere, it sounds a little off-putting. Who would gravitate to a way of life based on what sounds like nothingness? Like insights into not-self, insights into emptiness of the world can be unsettling.

"Those discourses dealing with emptiness" would be misunderstood and neglected, the Buddha predicted, yet sunyata was the apex of his teaching: there is (and has been) no arising (origination or creation), no abiding, and thus no perishing; while these appear to be real, they are empty of reality, they are an illusion.

In the Prajnaparamita Sutras, the Buddha taught:

> No beginning is perceptible,
> No end is perceptible,
> And nothing in between is perceptible either...
> Like a dream, like an illusion,
> Just like a city of fairies,
> So is arising, so is abiding,
> And so is destruction taught to be.

As Buddha said to a disciple in the Diamond Sutra,

> No beginning, Subhuti, is the highest truth!
> As a lamp, a cataract, a star in space
> An illusion, a dewdrop, a bubble
> A dream, a cloud, a flash of lightning
> View all created things like this.

## D.T. Suzuki:

> The first declaration made by Hui Neng, regarding his Zen experience, was that "From the first, not a thing is"; and then he went on to the 'Seeing into one's self nature', which self nature, being 'not a thing,' is nothingness. Hui Neng further argued: there are no forms to be recognized as such. Being so, there is no use in establishing anything.

So the first step in sunyata is the last, or only, step: where there has been no origination, or creation of anything, it is clear that all we perceive and suppose that we experience cannot actually be real or true; we are only present in a dream of our own dreaming. No forms of any kind are actually existing, or abiding: all forms are empty of ultimate reality. Since no forms exist in truth, what are some of the major points which this reveal?

The Dalai Lama:

> Emptiness is the nature, the final character, of form itself. The Tibetan sage Tsongkhapa quotes a passage from the Kashyapa Chapter in the *Pile of Jewels Sutra*. "Emptiness does not make phenomena empty; phenomena themselves *are* empty." When I was in Ladakh a year or so ago, I found a similar passage in the *Twenty-five-Thousand-Stanza Perfection of Wisdom Sutra*: "Form is not made empty by emptiness; form itself is emptiness."

Advaita emphasizes that "All is One"; ajata erases both the "All" and the "One" as definitional concepts. Any thoughts of "existence" are dependent upon sensate consciousness; the dead are devoid of both the ideational entities of the Self or of the self.

The marvelous point of ajata (or sunyata) is that the true nature of ultimate reality is that it is empty; complete, total, 100% emptiness. In emptiness, not anything ever actually comes or goes. What the dreamer perceives as coming and going (including oneself) is empty of reality: in emptiness not anything ever happens, in fact, because not anything has ever actually been created, from the start.

Jay Garfield:

> We are driven to reify ourselves, the objects in the world around us, and—in more abstract philosophical moods—theoretical constructs, values, and so on because of an instinctual feeling that without an intrinsically real self, an intrinsically real world, and intrinsically real values, life has no *real* meaning and is utterly hopeless. Without viewing the world as empty, we can make no sense of any human activity.
>
> Although we are dreamers living within the confines of our own dream, all that we need to know to be awake within that dream is that all that appears to us—including oneself—is as empty of true existence as is an illusion. This is the gift of Madhyamaka: it allows us to awaken to the truth of our hollow existence, and to not take life—or death—seriously.

# In Plain Words

*"Why am I finding it so difficult to understand emptiness?"*

The reason sunyata, or emptiness, can be difficult to undertand is because you take yourself to be real.

Therefore, thinking *yourself* to not be empty, you look around you and try to imagine how emptiness works.

But in a dream at night, you also take it for granted that you are real, and existing as a real person. And yet when you awaken, you realize that you, as a dream figure, were not real—nor was the entire environment you operated in then. Not any of that had true existence.

You will not understand sunyata without understanding that the entire universe—and the universe itself—is empty of reality, or true existence. And this includes *you*.

So an unreal you is looking around at an unreal universe, attempting to sort out what is real from what is not real.

The message of sunyata is that not anything is *not* empty of reality. An unreal viewer is not apart from the unreal universe she is viewing—just as in a *dream*.

You ask, "Who is dreaming the Dream?"

Is anything within the universe *real*? Is the Dream *itself* real? Is the *dreamer* real?

The universe appears, to the dreamer, to be real. The Dream the dreamer is living, within the (unreal) universe, appears to be real.

The dreamer himself, in the (unreal) Dream, appears to be real.

But being (within) an unreal Dream, in an unreal universe, the dreamer cannot be real.

The point is, the Dream is not real, the dreamer is not real, the universe these are in is not real. Do you not suppose that you are in this universe? You are not real. Who within the unreal universal Dream is asking this question? Will any answer to it be real, or true?

Once one is awakened and is "beyond" the Dream, it is realized that NO ONE has *actually* been the dreamer of the Dream. The Dream is unreal. The dreamer is unreal.

Not anything has *ever* actually *happened*. This is the message of emptiness, or sunyata.

Not anything has ever been originated, or born, from the start.

How do we know that? If anything had ever actually been created, or formed, it would have to come out of, or be created by, a condition that was ("previously") formless. A formless condition is an empty condition. Not anything whatsoever can come out of an empty formless condition. To those who are within the Dream it can *appear* to be otherwise, but what appears to be so to a dreamer is simply an element of the Dream.

When you close your eyes for the last time, the Dream will evaporate, as well as its dreamer; the entire universe will no longer appear. There will only be emptiness—which is all there is this very moment.

The message of sunyata is that "life" is not real; "life" is in the universe, and it is *empty* of reality.

Buddha states that those who "gain perfect clarity of mind" (enlightenment), "do not create the perception of a *self*. Nor do they create the perception of a *being*, a *life* ..."

"The Buddha said...Neither can someone who creates the perception of life [his or others'], or even the perception of a soul [or afterlife], be called a bodhisattva." He emphasizes, "No beginning [and thus no finite ending], Subhuti, is the highest truth...And thus does the Tathagata say, 'all dharmas have no self, all dharmas have no life, no individuality, and no soul'...Subhuti, this dharma teaching cannot be heard by (those) who mistakenly perceive *a self*..."

One who understands this (an "awakened") need have no concern about *anything*.

*People conceive of right and wrong as being opposites that truly exist. If we are not able to reverse this tendency (to think that right and wrong are truly existent) it will be impossible for us to realize emptiness.*

...

*However, in order to understand the true nature of reality, we must realize that nothing ever really happens. We must realize that arising and birth are not real.*

...

*When we gain certainty in the teachings on emptiness, however, then it will be impossible for doubt to arise.*

Tsultrim Rinpoche

## Co-Arising is No Arising

Where not anything has ever arisen, there is emptiness. What we presume is *not* emptiness is fabrication. Either we comprehend the ultimate condition of emptiness or else what we comprehend is simply fabrication.

"Dependent co-arising" is the *form* of "emptiness is form". While all forms are considered to have a beginning and an ending, not anything we regard as a form is self-standing, or self-created; a form may be considered to be a cause of something, or else an effect of some other thing. In fact all that we consider to be forms are actually a creation or *conception* by one *form* in particular, the human "mind". The point is that all forms are *dependent* for their presumed existence: all *things*, it can be said, are dependent on some other thing (or things) for their "arising"—your self included.

So all forms, dependently-arising as they are, have no "self-nature"; are not independently existing phenomena. In other words, each thing is empty of *reality* as a fixed entity throughout the passage of time: all things are transitory, mutable, dependent upon extraneous causes or conditions. In short, "form is empty" of reality.

That *emptiness* of reality is what form actually *is*. Emptiness itself does not "exist" (nor non-exist), we might say, "in a vacuum". It is what form is when we recognize that no forms can have self-nature. But if there were no appearances of forms, the emptiness of reality in forms would be meaningless. Thus, you might say, emptiness is "necessarily" the *being* of forms which (co-dependently) appear. Form is emptiness, emptiness is form.

Not anything could be less complicated than emptiness. However, we cannot "see" emptiness. What we think we do see, though, are appearances of (dependently co-arising) forms; and that which thinks it sees them is itself one: you.

Our idea of, our conception of, space is itself a form. Time is a related form. These are conditional (and, in us, conditioned) and mutable perceptions, differing circumstantially; and appearing to occur in time and space is our supposition of "cause and effect". Dependent co-arising is, itself, a conception based on a *cause* of the dependent arising, which presumably results in the *effect* of dependent arising: one thing "co" operates on the other thing.

But what one needs to bear in mind is that the "one thing" is as empty of reality as is the "other thing": both cause *and* effect are unreal conceptions in the (unreal) mind.

The cause-and-effect relationship (so-called) is particularly important for the spiritual seeker to understand. It has to do with ideas that *practice* leads to *enlightenment*.

The idea of cause and effect, or course, is the basis of our entire concept that birth leads to death. Where there has been "no arising", in the first place there can be no "passing away".

# Advaita meets Ajata

David Godman wrote a biography of H.W.L. Poonja, known as Papaji, who was awakened by Ramana and himself became a spiritual teacher. The three-volume work is titled *Nothing Ever Happened*.

Godman:

> From his own insightful experience, Papaji arrived at the conclusive perspective of ajata. Evidence of this appears in a 1982 letter Papaji wrote concerning a well-researched book he'd read about Guadapada, an Indian sage of advaita.
>
> Guadapada (6$^{th}$ C. AD?) wrote about ajata-vada: *a-jata*, non-being or non-manifestation; *vada*, teaching. This can basically be summarized as "nothing ever existed (or happened)." As Ramana once put it: "no reality or absence of it."

Godman prefaces Papaji's letter on Guadapada:

> He upheld the radical *ajata* position that nothing has ever been created. Papaji too maintains that this is the highest teaching and the highest truth, but he prefers to express it by saying, "Nothing has ever happened. Nothing has ever existed."

Papaji writes that Guadapada quotes from some earlier Madhyamika sages, such as the Indian Buddhist monk Nagarjuna:

> The main thing that Guadapada teaches in the *Karika* is the *unreality of the world* and its abso-

lute *non-origination* (*ajata*). The former is advocated by Vijnanavadins and the latter is proved by Madhyamikas. Guadapada has fully utilized these lines of thought and has expressed his complete agreement with their views.

The doctrine that there is no external reality is common to both Guadapada and Vijnanavadins. The world, according to both, is a figment of the imagination. There is no difference between the world of waking and the world of dreams. Both are enclosed within the body. Just as things imagined in the dream are 'seen' inside the body, the objects of the waking world also are inside the body for they are equally the product of imagination. Their appearance outside of us is but an illusion.

The external world is a vibration of the mind. The doctrine of non-origination (*ajata*) which Gaudapada advocates is essentially a Madhyamika view.

Nagarjuna's *Madhyamakakarika* begins with the words, "There is neither suppression nor origination." This doctrine is accepted by Gaudapada and he commends it to his followers....

Guadapada pays homage to Buddha in his works. He also agrees with the Madhyamika conclusion that *ajata* is the highest truth. All this is possible because the difference between Vedanta and Buddhism is very slight. Buddhism itself owes much to the *Upanishads*.

**Ajata is the final culmination of what is known in Buddhism as wisdom, but little is said of it. As Papaji has said, "There is something more to be done after complete and final realization, but I don't speak about it. I have never spoken about it, and I don't find it mentioned in any books I have read, even the ones authored by 'enlightened Masters.'"**

Summarizing his views, I will put together some statements Godman has recorded. Papaji:

> You have never allowed yourself to experience the emptiness that is empty of all objects. Instead have the conviction, "I am in emptiness right now. Emptiness is my nature." Nothing will be left—no gods and no *universe*. This is the same nothingness that must have *preceded* "the gods" and their "creations."
>
> Nothing has ever existed. This, ultimately, is the only truth. Whatever else you read in the scriptures comes from a different perspective, a relative perspective which assumes the reality of ideas such as birth, death, bondage, and so on.
>
> I will tell you the bare truth: there is no birth, there is no death, there is no creator and there is no creation. This is now my conviction, my experience. What is seen does not exist. I know the truth that nothing has ever happened.
>
> Nothing ever existed at all. No one exists, nothing exists. This is the truth. In reality, nothing has ever been created. Absolute non-manifestation is the only Truth. That place is my real home. It is where I always am. One can say this with authority only when one abides in that ultimate place where nothing has ever happened.

Godman says of "the essence of his most fundamental experience," Papaji himself has the direct knowledge that he was never born and that he will never die. There is no future for him at all, because he has understood that time itself is unreal. When the body that everyone has been calling Papaji finally stops functioning, nothing will happen to "him". He will just remain as *he* is, the formless unmanifest.

*Ceasing to take anything whatsoever, whether personal or non-personal, as real in its particularity, that is for us the way things are really.... Therefore it has been established that even nirvana does not exist.*

Chandrakirti

## No Attainment

Spiritual teachers, down through the centuries, have spoken of (what we might call) the condition of "emptiness." Where is one to turn today in order to learn the implications of this reported reality?

Go to the library and check out twenty or so volumes on the subject: you'll find that the preponderance were written by professors of philosophy (often as their doctoral dissertation) or by translators of venerable treatises in Sanskrit, Tibetan or Chinese.

Since Buddhism has long been a subject of interest to philosophers, the majority of these books focus on arguments between various (often extinct) sects' schools of thought, generally straying far afield from an exploration of the implications of emptiness. In other words, little of the material will be of value, in plain English, to a reader today.

The two pillars of Buddhism—the Heart Sutra and the Diamond Sutra—have been succinct, dependable sources on the general implications of emptiness, for millennia. Few there are who aren't familiar with the six-word summary in the Heart Sutra: form is emptiness, emptiness is form.

However upon learning this, as I did decades ago, one might superficially conclude, "This is just saying that form and emptiness are the same."

Yes...but the key is in recognizing that within that sameness there's an important difference.

Every form is impermanent, presumably has a beginning and ending in "time" and "space." Emptiness, itself, would be formless (which is why the contrast with form): no beginning anywhere, no ending anywhere.

This difference tells us something about the nature of what we take to be reality, and what only *appears* to be reality.

Appearances appear: they come and they go. Anything which we would properly call reality, as a presiding or ultimate condition, does not come and go.

If this is so, any ultimate condition would know nothing of beginnings or endings. Therefore that condition could not generate or propagate anything which does come and go: that is, forms of any kind; appearances of any sort. Forms, in their appearances, have no substantial reality, in other words; not any thing exists as it appears to.

What *are* these appearances, in reality? Empty. And what of emptiness itself? It can only be empty. Emptiness is the present condition, emptiness is the ultimate condition.

This sheds a different light on the complete teaching in the Heart Sutra. How does one "live" one's "life" where not anything can have lasting, meaningful importance? In fact, *is* there a "life," in actuality?

In the Samyukta Agama, Buddha says directly:

> What is the discourse on emptiness in its ultimate meaning? Monks, when the eye arises, there is no place from which it comes; when it ceases,

there is no place to which it goes. Thus the eye, being not real, 'arises'; having arisen it 'ceases' completely....

A noble disciple, observing things as they really are, sees that the world is empty. The world is empty: it is eternally, unchangingly devoid of self or of anything belonging to self....

Monk, all compounded things are as an illusion, a flame, ceasing in an instant, not really coming (or arising), not really going (or ceasing). Therefore, monk, you should know, rejoice in and be mindful of this: all *activities* are empty; empty of permanent, eternal status, unchanging nature; not-self-and-not-belonging-to-self.

## Sushila Blackman has written:

As Ninakawa lay dying, Zen Master Ikkyu visited him.

"Shall I lead you on?" Ikkyu asked.

Ninakawa replied: "I came here alone, and I go alone. What help could you to be to me?"

Ikkyu answered: "If you think you really come and go, that is your delusion. Let me show you the path on which there is no coming and going."

With his words, Ikkyu had revealed the path so clearly that Ninakawa smiled and passed away.

*We can continue to perform our daily activities, yet at the same time remember that the things we normally see do not exist.... Nothing exists other than emptiness.*

Kelsang Rinpoche

# Profound Wisdom

The heart of the Heart Sutra—which is the heart of sunyata—is simple (it can be printed on two pages). A conversation is held, in the presence of the Buddha, between a "venerable" disciple and an esteemed awakened disciple. Shariputra asks Avalokiteshvara to explain, "the profound perfection of wisdom." The response is succinct. ("A word to the wise is sufficient."–Cervantes)

> Form is empty. Emptiness is form. Emptiness is not other than form; form is also not other than emptiness. In the same way...consciousness is empty.
>
> Shariputra, likewise, all phenomena are emptiness; without characteristics; unproduced, unceased....
>
> Shariputra, therefore, in emptiness there is no form...no consciousness...no body, no mind... and no phenomena.
>
> There is no...aging and death. Similarly, there is no...origination.

Hearing this clear explanation of sunyata, Buddha "commended" Avalokiteshvara:

> Well said, well said...it is like that. It is like that... just as you have indicated.

Shariputra, like most people, may not have understood what he was being told. But, centuries later, an Indian monk (Nagarjuna) pondered such instruction and wrote a logical explanation of it.

The phrase, "there is no origination" is developed by the phrase "all phenomena are unproduced." (The word "phenomena" has its roots in a word which meant "to appear, as in fantasy". Here, it means whatever is apparent to one's senses.)

The universe is a phenomena; it is thought to comprise the cosmos and all other phenomena that are believed to exist.

But if all phenomena have not been produced, that would mean that not anything has ever actually originated, or been "created".

In other words, each phenomena takes its form, or "comes into being," in a manner apparent to the senses. But since not any phenomena—including the senses — has ever actually been produced or created, "form is empty" of existence, or reality: "form is not other than emptiness."

Scientists inform us that before there was the appearance of a universe, there was nothing. There was only emptiness, "the void".

This original lack of production is why Avalokiteshvara points out that in truth ("the profound perfection of wisdom") there are no bodies and thus no minds nor consciousness actually in existence: no you, nor phenomena other-than-you. "Form is not other than emptiness—without characteristics."

Avalokiteshvara also said something else of significance:

"Similarly, there is no suffering...". How could suffering be real, if there was no person (or "other" person)—or anything else—which actually exists, or has been "born"?

Since there has been no birth, or other origination, there is neither aging nor death (cessation).

This "perfection of wisdom" was clear to Buddha (see the Diamond Sutra) and to Avalokiteshvara, and to Nagarjuna and writers who followed him, such as Aryadeva, Chandrakirti, and Shantideva, to name just the historic principals. Why does anyone have difficulty with it?

It can be truly understood only by those who have the capacity to know that they do not actually exist. Once we can acknowledge that (as one does in Self-realization), we are not in a position of seeking "reality" by someone who does not really exist. How can such a "person" comprehend that they cannot have actually been "created" or "born"?

Therefore, if *they* exist, all that they sense must likewise exist, or be "real". The idea is that because I see a universe, I exist; because I exist, I see a universe. Convincing?

One exists in their universe in a dream at night; upon awakening, what has become of that universe, and the phenomena in it? The nature of *all* forms is that they are empty of reality, whether in sleep or awake.

"Appearances" are the way things *seem* to be; "an apparition or pretense". "Real" means "not seeming, pretended or fictitious".

The dream is an appearance, as are the unreal figures acting out within it. They have not ever actually existed in reality: they have minds and consciousness, are born and die.

What is impermanent cannot ultimately be real. And even the universe, scientists declare, is impermanent.

# No Creation: No Problem

What can be said about ajata? David Godman has brought together a few quotes, from Papaji (H.W.L. Poonja) and Ramana Maharshi (Bhagavan).

First, David's comments (Gaudapada was the teacher of Shankara):

> Gaudapada declared "non-creation" to be paramartha, the final truth, and Bhagavan endorsed this conclusion, saying that it tallied with his own experience. Papaji too sided with Gaudapada on the issue of whether creation "never happened."
>
> Ajata, flying in the face of logic, common sense, and everyday experience, says very clearly that not even an unreal, illusory projected world has been created. It sticks firmly to the position that there is no creation and no *causality*.... Something can only happen or exist if there is a knower, or an experiencer, of it. If there is no seer of the world, the world itself is not there, and never was...
>
> This is what certain masters have said on this topic, and I can add that they have all said this on the basis of their own direct experience of the Self.

And among the things said about ajata by Papaji:

> I have to accept Gaudapada's teaching. And that teaching is "Nothing ever existed at all"... If the ultimate reality is perfect in itself, then the act

> of creation can never be predicated on it....As a result, the whole world becomes illusory and non-existent. The world never did exist....You can see the world as real...or, like the Buddha, you can say that it is not there at all....It is the *names* and *forms* that never existed....Absolute non-manifestation is the only Truth.

And Ramana explains that ajata cannot be pictured by anyone who cannot envision total emptiness:

> ...they are told, 'God first created such and such a thing, out off such and such an element, and then something else, and so forth. That alone will satisfy this class. Their mind is otherwise not satisfied, and they ask themselves, 'How can all geography, all maps, all sciences, stars, planets and the rules governing or relating to them, and all knowledge, be totally untrue?'
>
> To such it is best to say, 'Yes. God created all this and so you see it'. All these are only to suit the capacity of the learner....One who is established in the Self sees this [ajata] by his knowledge of reality.

The understanding of ajata is at least as old as the Upanishads, but becomes clear to those who are most steeped in advaita.

What can be more difficult to comprehend than nothingness? Even the word commonly used as an alternate—emptiness—suggests something to be (or could be) emptied. In *nothingness,* there is not even *that* suggestion.

Nothing means *nothing*—and not even something which *became* nothing. It was (that is, *is*) nothing from the *start*; never not ever anything.

The importance of the understanding of ajata is its practicality. In nothing, there are not (nor can ever be) any "problems".

The sixth Chinese Zen Patriarch won his roshi's robes and begging bowl, according to legend, on the basis of a poem demonstrating his contemplation of emptiness. The last two (of four) lines of Hui Neng's poem:

> Where there is nothing from the start,
> How can the dust [confusion, problems] alight?

Of course, where there is nothing from the start, there is not even dust. No problems to "alight" anywhere, for anyone.

The Heart Sutra tells us,

> All phenomena are emptiness—
> they are not born.
> In emptiness, there is no consciousness
> no body
> and no mind.
> There is no form…no origin.

The Dalai Lama tells us,

> All phenomena are empty.
> Emptiness pervades the whole of reality.
> That emptiness is its ultimate nature.
> We project onto things a status of existence
> which is simply not there.
> The understanding of emptiness is one
> of the principal factors of the true path.
> Such an insight cuts right through the illusion
> created by the misapprehensions of grasping
> > *things* and *events*.

And I have written:

> In my estimation, any teaching which assists one

to connect with the reality of the sheer emptiness of their existence—in life *or* death—is a *practical* teaching.

Fortunately, we have the capacity to *realize*, while we are *alive*, that *ultimately* nothing really matters. Considering that (ultimately *nothing really matters*), how much anguish should we invest in our temporal, impermanent, "relative" fixations in the meantime?

It is *this* awareness which is the conscious state of the thoroughly Self-realized. As a consequence, his attention is merely on the *moment*, as one is when witnessing the unfolding of a *dream*.

Wherever he looks, and whatever he views, he sees only *impermanence*: emptiness—recognizing that he who *sees* is no less empty. "His" life, the world, the universe can cease to be—even to ever have *been*—at any moment.

This recognition, this awareness, dictates his every movement—every one of which holds the amusing "importance" of potentially being his *last*.

So, he has, in a sense, "Died before one dies," and his *absence*, or non-existence, is as much in his conscious awareness as is his momentary *presence*.

**In the emptiness after death, there will not even be anything there—as far as you are concerned—to pose such questions as, Does Nothingness exist or not exist?**

# The "Mystery"?

The nature of *ultimate* reality can only be understood when looking from its own viewpoint. That is to say, one's *conditioned* perspective of reality must be put aside.

The simplest explanation is to consider that one's life in the world and universe has the characterization of a dream.

Into this dream, each dreamer is born. To the dreamer, the world and universe have the appearance of being real. The dreamer takes himself to be real, and therefore the world and universe this person is "in" to be real.

The dreamer "knows" that he has "come into" this life, therefore at some point he will "go out" of life. The dreamer "knows" that although he will die, the world and universe and fellow dreamers will persists after his death; that the dream will continue when the dreamer no longer exists.

None of this is so. When the dreamer ceases to be, the *dream* ceases to be.

The dream has never been real. The dreamer has never been real. In other words, an unreal dreamer dreams a dream that is unreal.

Only if the person, the world, and universe were real

would any of this be justified to have an explanation. Any explanation would entail the process of cause-and-effect, time and space (or location). Ultimate reality has no relationship to time, space or cause-and-effect. These are elements which occur only within the dream.

Only within the dream is it a legitimate question to ask, "How then can life and the world and universe *be*?" Therefore, any answer will be an answer within the unreal dream.

The point is that all that is *apparent* to the dreamer is simply that: an illusory appearance. What *appears* to be real or actual is not the same thing as what *is* real or actual.

What *is* actual, is ultimate reality. Ultimate reality can be characterized as empty; no-thing or nothingness.

Ultimate reality is absent *any* of the qualities of the dream. Being emptiness itself, it has no need of an explanation or a justification. There are no questions which one can ask about nothing. Questions and answers are a product of the dream.

Nothing is not the *cause* of anything or the *effect* of anything. Cause-and-effect is a process only within the dream. So, if we ask, "What is the cause of the unreal dream?", the cause is the unreal dreamer. An apparent dreamer interacts in an apparent world in an apparent universe.

None of what *appears* to be is actual. What appears as "real" within the dream is not actual, not ultimate reality. To understand ultimate reality, one must go "outside" the conditioned perspective that is within the dream. It can only be understood from the standpoint that no *thing* is real. *Nothingness* is what's real.

From the standpoint of nothingness, it is clear that not anything in our dream world, including oneself, is important. None of the activities in the world matter "outside of" the unreal dream. There is no meaning in life, in an ultimate sense. Anything which is to be taken "seriously" is within the unreal dream. Whatever you do, or anyone else does (or doesn't do), does not matter in any real sense.

This insight is the freedom which one can experience within the dream. It is justified on its own terms.

*If someone says to contemplate the mind, the mind is basically a delusion. And because a delusion is the same as an illusion, there is nothing to contemplate.*

Hui Neng

## Emptiness is not Extra

There are things which we, as humans, do because we have been conditioned to do them since the time of our earliest memories as a child; we take these instilled behaviors for granted, without ever questioning them. These are the conventional aspects of our lives. For example, we take for granted that the objects we see (including our self) exist in reality as they appear to us.

Some people go beyond taking the appearances for granted, and ask such questions as: If the phenomena in the universe are *real*, why do they not remain lastingly unchanged? Or, considering the current condition of phenomena in the universe, is this the *ultimate* condition?

So, conventionally we take it for granted that the things in the universe are real, and yet we can ask if what we *assume* to be real is the actual condition of reality ultimately.

Through logical reasoning, the sunyata masters (for example Nagarjuna, Aryadeva, Chandrakirti, Shantideva, etc.) have determined that emptiness is the ultimate, fundamental reality; and that therefore all the *phenomena* which appear to us are actually empty of reality.

The universe and the contents of its phenomena are, in the context of reality, unreal. This is why Buddha proclaimed "Form is emptiness, emptiness is form". All the things we presume are true conventionally, are *true* only in the ultimate sense of their emptiness. And yet, what makes this conclusion paradoxical is that if we consider emptiness as an alternate of any form it imbues, this emptiness—as with any other *form*—must also be empty of reality.

In other words, if emptiness is considered as any other thing is *conventionally* considered, it too is simply another thing to which "unreal" applies.

Since emptiness is not simply another *entity* to be contrasted to the entity of form (which it does imbue), it does not arise *separately* from form; when form arises, it arises *as* emptiness. Emptiness is not "added on", as something *apart* from form. "Form *is* emptiness. Emptiness *is* form."

Likewise, when a form ceases, emptiness *ceases*. Emptiness does not have a form; apart from its existence *as* form, it does not exist—*emptiness* is empty of reality.

So, while we may speak of emptiness as the ultimate condition, total and complete emptiness is not in a position to be in any kind of "condition", ultimate or otherwise. Emptiness has to be utterly empty.

We speak, in conventional terms, of emptiness "existing" as form exists. (Yet form does not exist, because it is empty of reality.)

But apart from conventionally, emptiness does not exist in any way that we assume phenomena exist.

In other words, emptiness can be described as existing and *not* existing. (Forms, in truth, have never existed because they have always been empty of reality, or existence.)

The significant importance of the work of the sunyata teachers is that it makes clear to us that not anything (including emptiness) actually exists as it appears—and that, of course, *includes* us. An unreal person—empty of reality from beginning to end—looks out on an unreal universe.

In the words of perennial sages, not anything has ever actually happened: arising, decaying and subsiding are all fictional appearances.

The above explanation can help make clear the following:

> Nothing *exists* ultimately.
> Geshe Tashi Tsering

*Examine now this world of living beings:
Who is there therein to pass away? .... Thus
life passes quickly, meaningless.*

*When examined in this way, who is living
and who is it who will die? .... With no truly
existent benefit or harm, what is there to be
happy or unhappy about?*

Shantideva

# Change

> Last year,
> a foolish monk.
> This year,
> *no change.*
>
> – Ryokan Taigu

Garma Chang discusses another way in which one can understand the nonexistence of things. In our Dream world, change is an element: "All things change" (all the time), both objects and events.

Everything is changing, *moment* to *moment*. A *young* man does not grow old: the *old* man is *no longer* a young man.

Even if we were to assume an object or event had ever been created, or come into being, there is not a moment that it continues to exist as the object or event originated. Change is at work every moment on everything. In other words, there is no static moment in "duration", for anything. This is what "impermanence" means: no lasting reality. The very moment that something "is", is the moment when it no longer is; its "existence" is cancelled out.

In fact, "change" itself is a process which presumably takes place in time. Time, and therefore change, is no more real than the objects and events which are thought to appear in it.

That any thing appears to change shows that the thing is not self-composed, or independently free-standing. If there were such a self-reliant thing, it would be impervious to *effect* upon it. It would remain as it had presumably been originated, indefinitely, immortally. We know of no such thing.

And change itself is impermanent and subject to change (now faster, then slower etc.). Were change to stand still, it would not be change. So change does not "endure" either, and is simply another element in the impermanent Dream.

# How It Is/n't

All creation is a product of the mind, and not of a Creator. And what is created is the idea that a mind is a reality, an existence.

The mind creates the "self", which has a "mind". The existence of the self and the mind depend on each other. These create reality for each other, as well as for the "world" they inhabit. All of this is fabricated, as impermanent as a mirage; not truly existing, self, mind and the world have no independent origin.

When what we think of as the self "dies", the mind dies, the world disappears with it. There is emptiness. There was emptiness at the time the self, mind and world appeared: there is ever only emptiness; appearances themselves are empty.

What is thought of as the mind and self, cannot think of or envision its own *non*-existence. We think and believe the world is as "real" as the self (or that the self is as real as the world). But how real, when all can and will disappear? What can appear only as a dream, will disappear in the same way a dream disappears. If anything has been *truly* originated, it will not cease to remain. It's the mind which "creates" birth and death, and its "life" in between. What is the origin of this mind? It has no origin because it does not truly exist, nor does the self which it "inhabits"; nor the world which it inhabits; nor the universe which these inhabit.

Only nothingness ever remains—and that too is a thought, an idea by the mind. Not anything truly exists outside of emptiness. Is that the truth? The truth, when formed, does not exist apart from emptiness.

So, "live" this "life" knowing that you're not, really. Make your appearance in the illusory world, as you do in your sleeping dreams. When awakened from this dream of life, all there will be is emptiness, as always; no mind, no self, no other selves, no world or universe. Nor has there *ever* been, beyond the appearance, which has no more reality than a dream.

# Nothingness

Underneath the condition when you are awake and aware, and beneath the condition when you are in bed at night and dreaming, there is the deep-sleep condition. Here, there are no thoughts, there is no "you", no mind, no relationships, no other, nor world, or universe. There is merely a condition of empty presence, no-thing-ness.

Everything, every form, event, etc., is superimposed on this empty presence, by the mind in the waking or dreaming state. But the organism, the body, continues to exist despite these daily reoccurrence of emptiness.

This condition in which there is no mind, no thoughts, no forms, and no you, is the "ground" state, your natural state. This empty presence is the condition of the organism before its birth (and its conditioning and the arising of the I-thought), and will be its condition once again upon the death of the form of "your life".

In other words, an organism appears to arise within empty presence, matures, and recedes again into empty presence (similar to the way an electron arises and recedes in the quantum field).

The organism knew nothing of existence or nonexistence before birth, and will know nothing after death: "You" will not know that you— or *anything* else— ever had "existed".

Recognizing the fleeting temporality of "existence"—and that existence will be completely non-existent, in due course—it becomes clear that not anything that you do, think, feel or say has any lasting significance or meaning. (This is the message of the Bhagavad Gita.) All that appears, to the organism, to be done is merely a momentary expression of the field of ever-present beingness—utterly lacking in lasting reality.

So, this is why it is said, in the nondual writings, that "nothing really matters". It is also why it is said that (as a book about Papaji is titled) "nothing ever happened."

Hui Neng, the Sixth Chinese Patriarch, wrote (in the last two lines of his poem), "Where there is nothing from the start, how can the dust alight?" "Dust", in Buddhism, means confusion. In other words, where there is *nothing* from the start, where can *any* "problem arise"?

So, all that we learn in advaita is intending to point our attention to nothingness. (And not its "existence" or "nonexistence", since where there is *nothing*, neither of these are applicable.) In other words, the intention of advaita, or nonduality, is to direct us to ajata. And, I would say, a thorough understanding of the former is necessary in order to comprehend the latter.

Ajata *means* "no creation"—nothing from the very "beginning"; not *any* thing which can be conceived nor named: not *even* the "Absolute"—and certainly, no minds which could conceive of any thing. The word, in Buddhism, would be sunyata.

So when we come to recognize that, in truth, there is nothing from the start, we understand what is meant when it is said that all that we perceive is simply a dream, an illusion—seemingly superimposed on ever-lasting empty presence.

Now, is this information simply an interesting "analysis", or does this have practical value? Someone recently sent me a book by the Dalai Lama, and I'll extract a few quotes.

> All phenomena are empty. Emptiness pervades not only your individual ego or sense of self, but the *whole* of reality....That emptiness of *mind* is its ultimate nature, or mode of being. To *realize* that, is to pierce and see through the deception of ignorance...freedom from ignorance (is called) nirvana...
>
> Realizing emptiness is directly related to our quest to purify our mind of afflictive emotions like hatred, anger, and desire...We project onto things a state of "existence", and a mode of being which is simply not there....
>
> This understanding of emptiness..is one of the principal factors of the true path....For such an insight cuts right through the illusion created by the mis-apprehension of *grasping* things and events as existing....We *realize* the emptiness of *all* phenomena, not just the mind and body of the individual.

*Phenomena are not objectively existent and are only established as existing through subjective designations and thoughts....In short, it is said that though there is no phenomenon that is not posited by the mind, whatever the mind posits is not necessarily existent....If we become familiar with this, the objects viewed—self, other, and so forth—appear as illusion-like or dream-like falsities, which although not inherently existent, appear to be so.*

Dalai Lama

# Ultimately Nothing Exists

The things we take to be real are not, in truth, originated or established by their own will or right; this is an assumption we superimpose.

Among our false ideas is that the origination of things is an effect, for which there has been a cause. But if an effect is dependent upon a cause, causes are the consequences of prior effects. No cause or effect is self-generating. (This is what is known as dependent-arising.)

In a similar way, we perceive that an *agent* and his *actions* are distinct or separable phenomenon. But they too are dependently arisen.

That things do not originate as a consequence of cause tells us that they are not self-abiding in their own right.

And if things were self-existent, from where would come the appearance, and the need, for what we perceive as change?

What is dependently-arisen is empty of true self-existence. Our assumptions otherwise are the product of thought or conception.

The most difficult thing—yet most primal—for us to recognize is the unreality of the self. For the sake of promulgating the teachings, the self is referred to as *if* there were one, until it can become clear that the *idea* of the self is merely another erroneous thought.

So, when we go about recognizing and refuting appearances, we must not neglect to remember that the *self* is also another appearance to be refuted.

In fact, where there is no "I", what of "my mind" and "my thoughts"?

All identifications are imputed by thought, and what is merely imputed by thought ultimately has no more reality than a dream—*including* thought itself.

One takes oneself to be real, therefore whatever one cognizes is also taken to be real. But the *idea* of reality—or even unreality—is a *concept* which depends on the mind for its designation.

All *things* are conceptually conceived and designated, and thus are empty of real or true or inherent existence of an independent or self-standing or autonomous nature.

So it is by conventional conceptual designation that all things are given their *presumed* reality. But the one who now recognizes the falsity of the existence of these things is now recognizing that not anything exists in its place: emptiness.

When we recognize that we ourselves are empty—and therefore the mind itself is not a reality—what can actually be imputed that is real?

## Snuffing Out Nirvana

Those who seek *nirvana* come to learn that the word means "to snuff out," as one would snuff out a candle: it means to bring the "self" to an end.

The consequence is that when the idea of "me" has ended, the idea of all that is "not me"—that is, the world or universe, and all "other than me" that is in it—also come to an end.

When we've recognized that the appearance that we call "I" is false, we likewise recognize that every "you" is equally false. And it is this "I" or "you" which is the preceptor of its universe. An unreal "person" is perceiving the environment supporting it—which must also be false, or equally unreal.

So, it is not that the person and the world are the same one thing (the Absolute), as we originally conclude. Neither the perceiver nor the perceived have ever actually existed as a fact, apart from an illusionary appearance by an impermanent seer. Where neither the seer nor the seen has existed in reality, the two are indeed the same—but the "same" is not a thing, it is *nothing*. The "thing" that it is, as Buddhists put it, is *empty* of reality. That is to say, there is no person or world, in reality, which can transmute into an Absolute. It is an Absolute which permeates a universe that does not, in truth, have existence.

So, the "snuff out" of nirvana is to begin with the *self*, follow logic, and snuff out as well the *universe* of the self. The consequence is what is known as *emptiness*.

# Actions and Effects are Empty

Because we take our own existence to be real, we assume that whatever appears to us must *likewise* be real: that is, what appears to a fictitious "person" and the utter Truth, that lies beyond the appearance of that person, are the same.

When we come to recognize that the *appearance* of what is true and what is *actually* true are different things, we begin an investigation that leads to the discovery that what appears to be real—I and my universe—are actually empty of reality. This insightful realization concludes in what is experienced as nirvana—which means "to blow out," as one blows out a candle.

The emptiness scriptures, or Wisdom scriptures, speak of "two truths." The *conventional* truth is that I exist; after all, it appears that *I* am looking at this question of what is ultimate reality. The *ultimate* truth is that ultimate reality cannot be known by a person who is real only in a conventionally-held sense. Put another way, until you come to the conclusion that your existence as a person is empty of reality, you will not grasp that all "other" things are likewise empty of reality.

At this point of understanding, the usefulness of the two truths ends. What makes conventional truth conventional is that it is conceptual: every thing within it is there by way of conception, thought. *I* am because I *think* I am; every person is the subject of a conception, by one's self and/or others.

Therefore, when we *think* of emptiness, emptiness too is conceived within the realm of a conventional "thing": in this sense, it is simply another named form. The fact is, from the *ultimate* perspective, emptiness is empty of reality—as are *all* things.

And so it is with the two truths: any truth, itself, is in the final analysis a conception—whether a conventional truth or ultimate truth. We could say that from the standpoint of ultimate truth, ultimate truth is empty of reality.

The point of this realization is to come to the understanding that the ultimate condition is simply, totally and unambiguously *empty*: without attributes, dimensions in time or space, beyond such conceptions as existent or nonexistent. *Empty*.

That it is the ultimate condition means that all things which appear to be real or existent conventionally—which is *all things*—are, in their final truth, empty of reality.

But this is not to say that *instead* their true existence is that of emptiness. Whatever appears to us is instantly (or has always been) empty; but when that appearance ceases to exist, not anything remains or takes its place: emptiness does not *exist*, as an independent entity.

When we say that emptiness is empty even of emptiness, this is so that we will not reify emptiness as something which actually "exists."

So, from the second of the two truths, we do not say that emptiness—which we could say is "real"—exists. However in terms of the conventional truth, we do say that you and your universe—which are *unreal*—exist.

Speaking of the truth of emptiness, then, we are not positing that nothing exists, in truth (nihilism). Appearances do, in fact, appear to exist—to a *person* who does appear to exist (although neither are actually real).

We are not saying that the appearances have any reality; they are empty of reality. But neither are we saying that the (conventional) appearances do not "exist."

One of the major confusions for us is the idea of *cause* and *effect*. Both of these are notions, or conceptions. When we view some phenomenon as an effect—say, the world or universe—we are prompted to wonder, "What was its cause?"

When we recognize that all things are empty, it becomes clear that an empty cause can be the cause of nothing more than empty effect. When we have realized that the universe is empty of ultimate reality, we no longer question "What was its cause?"

Can a questioner who is himself empty of reality conclude a real answer?

So, when we recognize that the fundamental nature is emptiness—which is not anything other than empty—what is it that we can expect to "arise" out of that which is nothing but empty? This is why the scriptures insist that not anything can ever "die" because not any thing has ever been *born*.

This emptiness is not something which has been created, therefore it is not something which has an ending. Beginnings and endings are creations of our mind.

We "see" appearances, such as you and the universe, but we come to know that all that seems to exist is empty of reality: life—mine and yours—is like a dream. We live out our illusive "existence" in an illusive universe. The dial comes around and says 360°, but 360° is back at 0°.

# What's Your Problem?

The first notion that occurs in a child's body is that of existence. How can it know it? It concludes that its body is separate from objects around its body. The mind concludes "There is you, and everything else is not you". Is this mind, which deduces separation—*apart* from the self—drawing an independent conclusion regarding the self? No.

This self/mind identifies the not-self as the world. Are the world and the mind that *establishes* the world separate? No.

Self-mind-world are each taken to have existence, to be real. The mind, lacking substance, projects a self living in a world.

But what becomes of this "real" self/mind and its "real" world when a sleeping dream is present? And, the self and world that appear in a sleeping dream, what becomes of them when a dream ends?

A mirage takes on a real appearance, but in terms of real water, it is empty. An appearance *appears* to be real. It appears that we are born, live a life, and die. The appearances are not real; the appearances exist as *appearances* but they are empty of reality.

The self, its mind and the world it projects *appear* to be real, but are only appearances.

The point of this is that the self/mind struggles with problems in a world of its creation, which are not true: such as "Where will I 'go' when I die?"

When the "self" is a self-creation, from the start, where is its "mind" and the "world" that the mind identifies?

When these are seen to be empty of reality, what becomes of the self-mind-world's problems?

# Co-Dependent

*Even if all the consciousness were removed from the universe, wouldn't the universe still exist?*

Consciousness and the universe are co-dependent. If there were no universe, where would consciousness reside? And if there were no consciousness, what could be conscious that anything existed?

From the standpoint of sunyata, or ajata, both the universe and consciousness—not being stand-alone *independent*—lack (what Buddhists call) inherent existence: in other words, do not exist on their *own*. This means that, as with all other things, they are empty of reality—despite the appearance.

From this point of view, the universe and everything in it, including consciousness, has never actually known creation or origination.

For example, both the universe and consciousness are the subject of dreams at night; we would not conclude though that either was real, or existed beyond the dream.

So, consciousness is not an individual property that would be possible to extract from the universe, even if either one of these were a reality, or had ever been created.

That neither the universe nor consciousness are real is the subject of Buddha's Diamond and Heart sutras, among other points.

*Sentient beings do not exist, so no life force can be found either—these phenomena are like bubbles of foam and hollow banana trees, like illusions, like lightning in the sky, like water-moons, like mirages.*

Buddha

# No Mind, No Matter

From the standpoint of the *relative*, we can speak of such things as you and me, matter and energy, even of abstracts like time and space. We can consider all these things together and ponder, in science, such things as the Big Bang origin of the universe.

But if we take the viewpoint of ajata, it says that nothingness is the actual existing "condition".

When we try to imagine or think about "nothing", there is always *something* which appears to us. But despite what occurs in imagination, *nothing* is a void, absence, a total and resolute emptiness. There is no spirit or energy present, let alone matter. Emptiness is empty of time and completely empty of space.

It is empty of all the constituents which science could concern itself with, even the physical laws.

So, while the effort to understand the Big Bang, as the origin of the universe, is engaging on the relative level, there has never been the evolvement of a universe to *explain*, from the standpoint of ajata. Ajata asks: if there were no minds in the universe, what could be said to *exist*?

That "nothing" is the nothingness one can only *attempt* to envision.

*The awareness of "emptiness" is not a blank loss of consciousness, an inanimate empty space; rather it is the cognition of daily life without the attachment to it. It is an awareness of distinct entities, of the self, of "good" and "bad" and other practical determinations, but it is aware of these as empty structures. Wisdom is not to be equated with mystical ecstasy; it is rather, the joy of freedom in everyday existence. ....The apprehension of emptiness is a solution to all problems, not because "a solution" has to be found, but because the problems have ceased to be "problems".*

Frederick Streng

# World Illusion

You write, "To say that the world is an illusion seems to me to be a theory. Many people in the world are suffering. Do you think that you could convince such a person that his or her suffering is an illusion?"

When you close your eyes for the last time, what do you consider will be your conception of the "reality" of this world? Is it possible that, in the process of death, all forms will fall away from consciousness? What is the reality of the "world" in your deepest sleep? This, I submit, is the meaning of "the world is an illusion." And, in that same sense, there being no world, what then of the "reality" of suffering?

You say, "I want to perceive reality as reality, and illusion as illusion." Both will disappear as distinctions, it would appear, at death—as they do in deep sleep.

What would your awareness consist of if you were to dismantle your tendency to consider matters in terms of "should" and "should not"? In your deepest sleep, is there anything which you conclude "must be" or "must not be"? When you draw your last breath, what will become of these ideals you have, concerning some preferable state of awareness?

Whatever state of awareness is *present* is "reality." Any desired state of awareness which is not present (but "should be") is nothing more than an idea *about* awareness, an "illusion" in the definitional sense—"not in *accord* with the facts."

# Awakening from the Dream

Were there such a thing as ultimate Reality, it would not be impermanent, it would not come and go; in other words, it would be without a beginning or an ending. This means it would not be *caused* by any other thing, nor would it be affected by any other thing; it would exist entirely independently, alone.

Every thing in the universe—and including the universe itself; that is, *every* phenomena and event—is purported to be impermanent, to have a beginning and ending. None of these exist *independently* of every other phenomena or event. Thus, ultimately, none of these forms have the characteristic of being finally real. Despite any *appearance* of being real, they lack the qualities of *being* real.

It is for a human mind that this distinction has importance. But the human mind—indeed the human itself—is not ultimately real. Can anything which *appears* to an unreal mind be real?

At night, you (your mind, that is) dream that you buy a car. The you, in the dream, has no actual reality: what, then, of the car that appears to it?

So "life", in this universe, is like an illusion, or like a dream. Not any part of it is real, beyond the impermanent appearances. To express this, the Heart Sutra has propounded the formula, "form is emptiness"—meaning that all phenomenon are *empty* of reality, or actual existence.

When all that exists in the universe (and including the universe) is unreal, has any of it had an *actual* beginning; in other words, has any thing ever actually been created, or caused or originated? The obvious answer is no.

Ultimate reality can have no beginning or ending. What has no beginning or ending is not itself a form; it is form*less*, or formlessness. (Neither does it have any relation to time, cause and effect, or space, which are—unreal—elements of our Dream). What has no form has no content; it is empty of all qualities and quantities.

Out of the ultimate condition of emptiness not anything can arise, or be originated; no *causes* are included within *emptiness*. So, from the ultimate condition, not anything has every arisen or been created.

In fact, not anything has ever actually happened, or occurred, at all.

Not anything that ever "happens" in "this life" has any meaning or importance at all. Nothing that you do (or don't do) matters ultimately.

The value of this knowledge is that it awakens us to the fact that not anything—you included—has every actually been "born" (aside from that appearance within the Dream of "life") nor, therefore, will ever actually die, or "lose" its (unreal) life.

This is to *awaken from* the Dream (while still "in" it), or to "see through" the illusion.

**In 25 words:**

All that is,

exists within the Dream.

You are within the Dream;

Simply be as you are.

Not any thing is real —

Ultimately, nothing matters!

*Subhuti, what the Tathagata speaks of as 'streams of thought' are no streams. Subhuti, a past thought cannot be found. A future thought cannot be found. Nor can a present thought be found.*

Buddha

# After "Death"

Thanks for your letter.

Your friend is right. When we close our eyes for the last time, there will be only emptiness. "You" will vanish, your world will vanish, the universe will vanish.

How can one know this? Because there is only emptiness right *now*. You, as who you think you are, are not real; therefore the world and universe that you perceive are not real. Not any thing we perceive is existing in the way in which it appears to us.

When you wake up from a sleeping dream, everything in the dream disappears. What is true in the sleeping dream does not cease to be true once we have awoken into our daytime life. This life while we are awake is simply a continuation of the dream while we are asleep.

In other words, the sleeping dream and the daytime dream are both within what I call the Dream with a capital D. You are in both dreams, and you are the "dreamer" of the one continuous Dream. You are not real, nor are the dreams that you are dreaming.

When the big-D Dream ceases for you, you won't even know that you have ever "existed" (which you haven't); just as when the sleeping dream ends, you no longer experience the "you" in the sleeping dream as existing.

The moral is, it makes no difference what you do (or don't do) in this life: not any part of it has any reality.

*Since the actor can exist only if there is an action, but the action can exist only if there is an actor, they exist only in mutual dependence, and therefore they have no nature of their own. They do not truly exist.*

Tsultrim Rinpoche

# Hard As a Diamond

When we look up at the sky and say "Look, there is a rainbow," we are alleging that a rainbow exists. Yet a rainbow is actually an illusion, so it is as an illusion that a rainbow exists. A rainbow as anything other than an illusion does not actually exist. So one can say that a rainbow exists and one can also say that a rainbow does not really exist.

It could be said that a rainbow near an unreachable mountain waterfall neither *exists* nor does *not* exist if no one has ever seen it and pondered either its existence or non-existence. In other words, the supposed reality or non-reality of any phenomenon is an assertion of a mind capable of such a discrimination. Outside of the mind, that is, there is not anything that can be determined to be either real or not real.

A mind considers that *it* is real; and being real, that whatever it determines is real *is* real.

Thus, the mind itself is real, the self which is the subject of the mind is equally real, and the world and universe that the mind professes to sense is likewise real.

What if there were no minds in the universe; would there be anything that was described as a universe; would there be any notions of a world; would anything identify itself as a self? Would anything be determined to be real or not real?

As it is, you *seem* to be a self; you seem to have a mind; you and your mind appear to see a world. But when you go to bed at night, that same you appears in a "real" dream world. While *engaged* in that experience, you do not deny it as "unreal". When awake, there is that "you" seemingly engaged in a "real" world, appearing to that very *same* mind.

Where a mind is not real, can any products of that mind be real? Would the self that's in your mind be real? Where the self is not real, would any thing which is *other* than the self be real?

We could say that all these appear to be real: they are real as *appearances*; like an illusion by a magician sawing a woman in half is real as an illusion—but recognized to be false when minutes later the woman takes a bow.

What this tells us is that if things are *not* as they appear to be—"real"—they are *not* real.

The key to what is *ultimately* real, or always real, is that which is not ephemeral, which does not change. The self changes, the mind changes, the world changes, the universe changes: all phenomenon have a *beginning* and an *ending*, and—even if there were not other differences—the difference between the two mark a change.

All forms have a beginning and an ending; forms change. That which is without a beginning and ending would not be a form; it would be form*less*.

What is formless would not be an entity, a thing: it would be no thing: nothing. Nothing—not a thing—does not change.

Nothing does not *exist*, except in our efforts to contemplate or describe it. Hence it does not *not* exist in that sense.

Whatever is without a form has no edges, borders, boundaries or perimeters. Being formless, it contains no content; formlessness is a zero, it is empty or void. In formlessness there is not any thing which can have an existence. To this extent, formlessness *itself* cannot be said to manifest existence.

In fact, in its emptiness it is absent any such identity as existent or non-existent. It is uncaused, uncreated, "unborn". Without any such characteristics as having a beginning or an ending, emptiness is without an origin and without a cessation.

Only one thing could be said of emptiness, if anything. Emptiness is utterly empty.

Thus it says in the Heart Sutra, to Buddha's approval, "Form is emptiness, emptiness is not other than form."

Form (including our own bodies) appear to us to be "real", but they do not actually exist in the way they seem to. Emptiness is the true nature of apparent forms and phenomenon. This is why the sages compare our life in the world to a dream or an illusion. Buddha, for one, declared:

> As a lamp, a cataract, a star in space,
> an illusion, a dewdrop, a bubble,
> a dream, a cloud, a flash of lightning—
> view all created things like this.

The first book ever printed—in 868 AD, on a Chinese press—was the Diamond Sutra.

Bill Porter (Red Pine) has written one of the 20,000 commentaries on the Diamond Sutra during the past 24 centuries. Buddha was so concerned for his teachings on emptiness, Porter says, that he told his attendant Ananda: "If you should forget all other teachings you have heard me speak, that would be a minor fault. But if you should forget but a single verse of this perfection of wisdom, that would be a serious fault, and it would displease me greatly."

"No beginning (no origination)," Buddha said in the Diamond Sutra, "is the highest truth." He says that no one who is onto this truth, "creates the perception of a self, a being, a life, or a soul….these forms are only names; these feelings, discriminations, compositional factors, and consciousness are only names."

The Ashtavakara Gita says of the universe:

> The universe itself is a figment of imagination. The universe, even though it seems present to the senses, is unreal. The universe does not in reality exist. This manifold universe is nothing…nothing exists.

So, all phenomenon—material or immaterial—are "real" only inasmuch as they *appear* to be real; in actuality, they are empty of real existence. This means that you and your mind appear to be real, but are not.

You and your world are projections of the mind, and the mind itself is not real.

It's not that the self, the mind, and the world have existed, and have been emptied out: not anything has ever truly existed from the start. Emptiness is—and being without a beginning, always has been—*the* condition. Period.

Yes, there are what *appear* to be phenomenon of solidity, but such appearances are utterly without a foundation in reality. *All* is empty.

This means that the passage of time, as well, is an illusion. Not anything actual can ever be produced out of emptiness, neither a beginning nor an ending. Not anything has ever been born or created, therefore not anything has ever actually died. Birth, life and death are non-existent. Not anything moves, in emptiness.

Despite what appears—to an apparent mind which has never existed in reality—not anything has ever happened.

Does anything then, in truth, really matter? No.

*When the recognition dawns that although things appear to be solid and autonomous they do not exist in that way, this indicates that you are really arriving at an experiential understanding of emptiness. This is known as perceiving things as illusion-like....Emptiness is therefore both the means of eliminating the mental afflictions (confusion) and the resultant state that one arrives at after having done so.*

Dalai Lama

# The Big Question

To answer your question from the standpoint of ultimate reality, it doesn't matter what you say, feel, think or do: "you" are not the doer, as the advaita teachings say, because you do not exist as you think you are—a separate individual.

So, does it matter if you save a (separate) "life"?: no; as there is no you who has a life (as Buddha says in the Diamond Sutra), there are no lives, separate or otherwise.

The most refined, or deepest, investigation of advaita is known as ajata. Ajata teaches (as do I, at my website ajatasunyata.com) that our so-called reality is an illusion. We are dreamers, living in a dream: the dream has no reality, in any ultimate sense. We ourselves are *within* the dream; we are no more real than the dream itself. In other words, not any thing which occurs in this "universe" or "world"—good, bad or neutral—is actually real, or true. So, does it *really* make any difference what we do? No: no more so than any difference it makes as to what is done in a *sleeping* dream.

In the big Dream, which occurs while we're awake (in particular), we are conditioned to presuppose that certain things "exist", in addition to ourselves: such as time, space and cause-and-effect, even life or death. As dreamers within the Dream, these things which we are conditioned to believe exist—such as, for instance, "I" and "death"—shape the nature of our Dream. As a dreamer, "I" will suppose, for instance, that "life" (especially mine) has a higher value than "death" (especially mine). Therefore, one will consider it most sensible to "save lives". But not anything which occurs in the Dream has any actual reality.

So, to answer your question, in the Dream you will, or you will not, attempt to save someone's life. Apart from (or "outside" of) the unreal Dream, it makes no difference what you do, or do not do. Not anything within the Dream has any reality, from an ultimate standpoint.

As the Buddhists put it, every thing within the illusion which we call life, and this universe, is "empty of reality". Likewise, anything beyond (or "apart" from) this illusive life and universe is equally "empty of reality". *Ultimate* reality is "emptiness".

In *emptiness*, not anything matters. In fact, in emptiness not anything has ever actually happened or occurred. Why? Because from emptiness, not anything can actually ever have originated or "arisen". This tells us *why* "life" is a dream of an unreal dreamer within the unreal Dream.

# Goodness/Evilness

Write co-authors JeeLoo Liu and Douglas Berger:

> The sage "forgets," as it were not as the result of any deliberate effort in suppressing emotion or desire. Rather, forgetting affectivity is an intellectual feat, resulting from the abandonment of judgement of what is *right* or *wrong*, for oneself.... If things are fundamentally derived from, and will ultimately return to, the state of nothingness or non-being, then our temporary existence, along with its sorrows and joys, should no longer be our primary concern.

So, the awakened recognition that the appearance of cosmic phenomena are in truth empty of reality is, to the sage, more than simply an interesting revelation: it is a shift in perspective which illuminates a renewed view of one's existence itself. The "reality" that one had previously taken for granted is now recognized as illusion. Where "I" had stood before there is now a view of emptiness, in fact an empty cosmos. In a condition of complete emptiness, there are no such qualities as gain or loss, sorrow or joy, or right or wrong—though these appear to be real to those who assume their *own* reality.

Regarding this, the Buddha is reported to have stated that those who "gain perfect clarity of mind" (enlightenment), "do not create the perception of a *self*. Nor do they create the perception of a *being*, a *life*..."

> The Buddha said...Neither can someone who creates the perception of a life [his or others'], or even the perception of a soul [or afterlife], be called a bodhisattva. And thus does the Tathagata say 'all dharmas [realities] have no self, all dharmas have no life, no individuality, and no soul.... Subhuti, this dharma teaching cannot be heard by [those] who mistakenly perceive a self'...

The point made by Hajime Tanabe echoes that of the Bhagavad Gita. The co-authors again:

> Tanabe's philosophy of nothingness is indispensable for us today. Tanabe's philosophy situates nothingness within the historical world of religion, politics, and individual practice, and acknowledges that radical evil is a necessary condition of existence in that very world.

> > According to the Madhyamaka teaching, all beings, including self and things, are empty in themselves. The same teaching also applies to the case of murder—the one who kills is empty in himself, and the victim who is killed is also empty in himself. Even the killing itself is empty in itself. This is therefore the same as saying that murder is empty in itself. There is no one who kills, nor one who is killed.
> > – Chen-kuo Lin

> Lin suggests that on the realist reading, *emptiness* is taken to be absence of agency, absence of the self, absence of the doer and the doing, and even absence of existence. Therefore, in the case of violent death, both the murdered and the victim are *empty*: there is no one who harms or is harmed—the good, the bad, the victim, and the assailant, are all empty.

Jay Garfield comments: "The ultimate truth is that *every-*

*thing* is empty; that nothing is ultimately *real.*" This is the operation of emptiness in the life of the awakened sages for whom both abundant goodness and radical evil are the same—empty of reality.

*We should perceive that everything—whatever may be said—is empty by its nature. So-called emptiness is empty too, and therefore there is nothing that's not empty.*

Nagarjuna

# The Unreal

As Ramana would point out, we need not try to explain something which is not real in the first place. Ajata says that not any thing has ever been created, from the very beginning. Any thing which could take on the appearance of having been created would therefore not really exist, in truth; it would be an illusion.

Let's examine such a situation, using an analogy. Picture that you are asleep and dreaming. In the dream, a baby is born and you understand that it is you: you are living in a world that is part of a universe. There are other people, there are objects in the environment, there are events, and you are conscious of what takes place internally and externally. Time, space, cause and effect are present.

In this dream, you are now a child. You are in a car with your parents, on your way to San Diego to attend the funeral of an uncle. So, even death is in this dream.

You wake up. All of this panorama was a product of your mind; its creation was entirely within the mind of the dreamer; not anything in it was a substantial or concrete reality. Though an illusion, it appeared to be true. If asked, you would not have denied that you were real, in a world that existed.

Now that you are awake: if asked, you would not deny that you are real, nor that the world and universe you are in truly exist. So, what could be called the big Dream (with a capital D) is the Dream in which your "reality" in a sleeping dream is not substantially different from your "reality" when you are awake. Neither exists, in truth, apart from your mind, or consciousness.

Where not any thing has actually ever been created, from the start, this would include the universe, the world, you, your mind, any thing, even time, space and cause and effect. Thus, birth, life, and death are not truly real. Not anything exists, beyond the appearance of existing. An illusion is "real" as an illusion, but it is not real beyond its *appearance* of being real.

So, in the big Dream, the dreamer himself is not apart from the Dream, he is within the Dream. The dreamer in an unreal Dream, who is himself equally unreal, is not in a position to ask about reality.

But what can be said is this: everything within the sleeping/waking Dream has no ultimate reality, beyond its appearance. If there were anything which could be said to actually be true, it would have to be beyond, or "outside" of, the Dream. In other words, from the standpoint of the Dream or its dreamer, it would have to be a *negative*: void, nothingness, emptiness. That is to say, reality would be on the other side of what is not real. Put another way, it would be something which does *not* make an appearance.

As Ramana said, we do not need to explain that which has no reality, the Dream and its appearances. But when we awaken from this Dream illusion, it will be clear to us that not anything which occurs within this Dream really matters ultimately.

What is ultimate reality is outside of the Dream, and that would be a void. A state in which not anything has been, or could be, created would be utter emptiness.

*When you practice expanding love and compassion, keep in mind that love and compassion themselves and the persons who are their objects are like a magician's illusions in that they appear to exist solidly in and of themselves but do not. If you see them as inherently existent this view will keep you from fully developing love and compassion. Instead, view them as like illusions.*

Dalai Lama

## Be As You Are

Taking yourself to be more than an appearance, you assume your world is also real, and more than an appearance. But a non-existent you, can only be seeing a non-existent world.

We establish a presumed universe, and then ask "How can we say that this is a void?"

Impermanence means that everything is in change constantly, moment by moment. No thing, in fact truly exists as a fixed "thing", at any time.

If there is a time that had a beginning somewhere, then time can come to an end. Time, then is not a lasting reality.

Since you do not exist, you cannot ask, "How am I here?", because in reality you aren't.

You appear to be real, to an unreal you—as the you in a dream takes its reality for granted.

If you were in *deep* sleep, where "you" and your "mind" do not appear, and the heart stopped: would you know that you had died?

Come to know that there is no death, and therefore nothing after it (especially a sensate "individual") and you will end such questions as "what comes after death?"

An actor can have the knowledge that he is not real, and that the character whose role he is playing has never been, and yet he can play out the role as his life.

When you close your eyes for the last time, this will all disappear. The slate will be wiped clean. You may say, "But it will be there for others". No: the 'others' disappear with 'you', not anything remains. So is the world real, or did it appear when you opened your eyes—and ends when you die? If the world is not real, are you real?

You say the mind is real because we both experience it. No, if it were real we would both have the same experience of the mind. And if the world were real, we would both have the same experience of the world. Anything that's real must be real to both of us in the same way.

Since there is no self, there is no mind. And because there is no mind, there is no perception or consciousness of a world or universe. "No mind" is the consequence of the realization of emptiness.

Emptiness tells us that there's not anything we need to get. Anything we could get would be empty. The getter itself is empty. Where there is nothing we need to get, there is nothing we can become. All that could remain is to be as you are—empty.

# Asleep or Awake

You are nothing....You may be totally unaware of this emptiness, this nothingness, or you may simply not want to be aware of it; but it is there, do what you will to avoid it....whether you are asleep or awake, it is always there....You and nothingness are one; you and nothingness are a joint phenomenon, not two separate processes....When there is the discovery, the experiencing of that nothingness as you, then fear completely drops away.

– Krishnamurti

After extensively reading Eastern and Western spiritual teachings, I thought I understood the words quite well but I wondered why I could not live the teachings, and why my life had not fundamentally changed. Recently, a deeper understanding of the teachings has significantly changed my perspective on life. While pondering J. Krishnamurti's statement, "You are nothing" (no thing), from his *Commentaries on Living*, I saw how I had been deceiving myself. For some 40 years I had been trying to understand the great spiritual writings, and going to countless dialogues of spiritual enquiry, thinking I could fundamentally change myself. My mistake was that I was subconsciously harboring a sense of myself as being a real entity....I was unconsciously identified with a mind that could only know what was limited, yet I was using it to try to know what was unlimited. I saw the confusion in myself and others was that the very *self* that was so knowingly expressing itself in dialogue was in fact a structure that could never "know" the truth.

– Vern Dvorak,
Ojai, California

*Q. Suppose a man were all of a sudden to make his appearance here and cut your head off with a sword. Is this to be considered real or not real?*

*A. This is not real*

*Q. Pain or no pain?*

*A. Pain too is not real.*

*Q. Pain not being real, in what path of existence would you be reborn after death?*

*A. No death, no birth, and no path.*

Ling Chiao questions Hui Chung

## Emptiness is Nothing to Fear

Thank you for your written report of your "first real taste of nonduality."

As you stated: "It's extremely simple....There are NO THINGS."

Each and every *thing* (whether material or immaterial) is a creation of the mind. Were there no minds in the universe, to dissect it into separate "things", there would be but a singular unbroken whole. Were there no minds, there would be no *names* given to supposed *forms;* there would be, simply, *no thing* (or nothingness).

Every form has a beginning and end; thus, is impermanent. Nothingness has no form; has no beginning or end; is formless. What you perceived is the ubiquitous "shared nothingness" of all seemingly-real objects. All objects are dependent upon their formless actuality for their appearance. All objects are limited, and appear "within" the unlimited formlessness; not one thing has ever been independent of it. All *things,* as you said, are "conceptual superimpositions" on a "universal" empty background.

Among the (immaterial) named forms is "consciousness" which, as you said, "creates" the relative appearance, the forms (naming each thing separately). Even consciousness itself is actually another empty object. All *things* come and go; only the ever-present emptiness remains, forever present and unmoving.

So, there is no need to cling to or attempt to repeat this awakening experience. You have only to know that the underlying actuality, to all that we claim exists, is nothingness. One goes on living one's life as an actor in a play: he knows that his "role" is unreal, and so he does not take his character (or that of others) too seriously.

*And* your fear is normal and natural, as well as temporary, when we move from the known (dualistic perspective) to the unknown (nondual perspective). When you recognize nothingness, you recognize that there cannot possibly be anything to fear in ultimate reality.

# Endnote

The endnote for the most sophisticated spiritual teachings, ancient through modern, is the final or ultimate revelation: emptiness from the beginning. In other words, out of the initial condition of emptiness, not anything has ever actually been originated.

In order to prepare the enquirer for this realization, it is necessary for him to recognize that even if there *were* such an existent entity as a universe, the universe and *every* thing within it is actually, itself, empty of any true reality.

Understanding the unreality of what we (ourselves unreal) *presume* is real is a teaching subject of Geshe Tashi Tsering, contrasting what appears to be true with what is actually true—"true" meaning empty of reality.

> Our reflection in the mirror isn't our real face; the echo isn't our real voice, the person we make love to in a dream isn't our real lover. To us they seem illusions. On the other hand, the world we live in—our body, our possessions, the buildings and streets of our town—seem to be very real. It is difficult for us to understand that they do not exist as they appear to us....
>
> We need to let go of that sense of *concrete* reality and see all things as illusion-like. To understand this discordance between appearance and reality requires an understanding of emptiness. Only with such an understanding will we be able

to see that *appearance* is the sense of intrinsic *existence*, whereas *reality* is the *lack* of intrinsic existence.

We each have been conditioned to assume that phenomena that appear to us are truly existent: this is our *convention*. But *all* appearances are in truth illusions; their *ultimate* reality is that they have no unconditional, or eternal, existence.

> ...all *conventional* truths are unreal in that they are all falsities. There is no actual "truth" in the nature of conventional truth....the face and the reflection of the face in the mirror are *both* deceptive, because they both *appear* to be inherently existent. Therefore, *both* are "unreal.".... Therefore, it is vital to be aware of how things actually exist, on the one hand, and how we misread reality, on the other, in order to correct our delusions.

### Tsongkhapa:

> "Convention" refers to lack of understanding, or ignorance: that is, that which obscures or conceals the way things really are....Since things must be mutually dependent, the meaning of "untrue" is that they do not essentially have the ability to stand on their own....The respect in which *ultimate* truth is a truth is that it is nondeceptive.

### Geshe Tashi Tsering explains further:

> A conventional or concealer truth—this "truth that conceals"—creates a fictitious world that works for us on a certain level....The world we know through conventional truths appears to give some degree of comfort and stability, but in reality it brings us difficulties....Life, feeling and communication only *seem* to happen within the sphere of relative truth, so does that mean that ultimate reality is nothingness?....I can see, feel,

and function. I can communicate, I can conceptualize...we feel we can easily distinguish between reality and fiction. Nevertheless, at one level it is *all* fiction. Our "real" world might cause us pleasure or tears that somehow seem on a different level from the pleasure or tears of a soap opera on television causes us, but at another level they are both fiction....Book, writer and writing all still appear to the consciousness as having intrinsic reality, whereas in reality they do not.

All phenomena—even a universe—have the characteristic of their impermanence. Anything which could be said to have been born must die; in the interim, not anything has a static, reliable existence.

> We all share this illness of fictionalizing the world we live in. All suffering arises from this misapprehension, and if we can see this, we will stop ascribing good and bad....There are many cultural things good or bad, right or wrong, that are believed to exist but in reality do not....Whether something is a material object or a mental event, whether it is useful or garbage, if that thing is created through causes and conditions, then it is impermanent....

> Although at a gross level impermanent things appear to arise, abide and disintegrate sequentially, at a subtler level there is no such sequence. There is no single moment in the existence of an object when it is not in the process of disintegration on a subtle level; at the very moment of coming into existence, it disintegrates. Thus, because the coming into existence and the disintegration are simultaneous, there is no time in which a phenomenon stays static...impermanence means *changing moment by moment.*

What is true must be actually, eternally true—even if there was no consciousness anywhere in the universe.

So the first thing we recognize to be untrue is our self, body and mind.

> Unanalyzed, the body instinctively appears to us as a single causeless entity, whereas when we do analyze it, we see that it is nothing more than a label placed on a collection of constantly changing parts, each a product of causes and conditions—and so it lacks any true, concrete, inherent existence whatsoever. Understanding that my body is impermanent will immediately stop my grasping at it as permanent, because these two are mutually exclusive phenomena.

As a result of recognizing that the true nature of everything is its ultimate emptiness, our ultimate realization is that even emptiness must be empty of existent truth.

> There is no more analyzing, because our mind resides firmly in the awareness of emptiness. This is the direct realization of emptiness, where there is no awareness of an "I" who is thinking "emptiness" but only emptiness itself....The table is the *base*, and the emptiness of the table is its ultimate truth. For emptiness, there is emptiness as a base; but then we must also posit the emptiness of emptiness as its *ultimate* truth. That emptiness base serves as the *conventional* truth to the emptiness of emptiness that is the *ultimate* truth.... When we have developed sufficiently and can perceive emptiness directly, we will be able to see all things as lacking inherent existence, and hence will no longer "see" things as existing inherently....Check for yourself. Do you live your life as if everything in your *world* lacks intrinsic existence? Are you totally free from clinging to things and events?

And even more importantly, are you aware that "life" and "death" too are empty of ultimate reality?

# Coda

The monographs in this book represent about a third of those available on my website ajatasunyata.com, with new writings still being added there.

The major historical madhyamaka writers (principally Nagarjuna, Aryadeva, Chandrakirti and Shantideva) are available in translations and you can find their source material online.

Centuries ago, as Buddhism was being crowded out of India, a treasury of sunyata material was transferred to Tibet; Tibetan Buddhists do much of the teaching on that subject today. Geshe Tashi Tsering is a highly readable author. Others inlcude: Khenpo Tsultrim Gyamtso, Geshe Kelsang Gyatso, Thrangu Rinpoche, and the Dalai Lama.

Two Western writers to read are Jay Garfield and Guy Armstrong. But interest in the perspective of emptiness continues to grow with new works being published every year.

*Since there is no longer an abyss,
where could one go astray?*

*In the experience of yogins who do not
perceive things dualistically, the fact that
things manifest without truly existing is so
amazing they burst into laughter.*

Longchenpa

www.ingramcontent.com/pod-product-compliance
Lightning Source LLC
Chambersburg PA
CBHW051132160426
**43195CB00014B/2443**